The LORD is my SHEPHERD

Psalm 23

Published by Kingdom First Books
kingdomfirstbooks@gmail.com

ISBN 978-1-5272-8454-8

The LORD is my SHEPHERD

Psalm 23

Illustrated by

Sara Lewis

The LORD is
my shepherd;
I shall lack nothing.

He makes
me lie down in
green pastures.

He leads me
beside still waters.

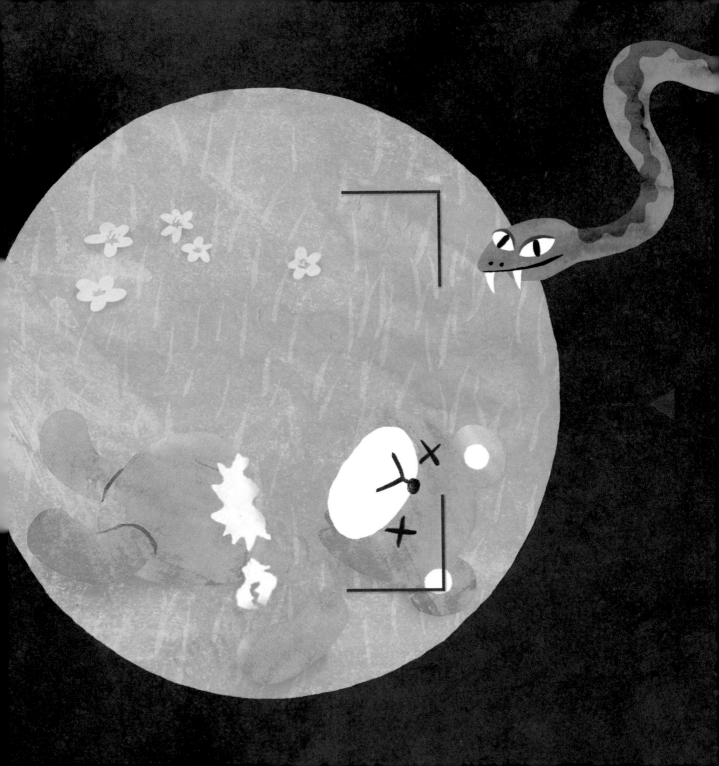

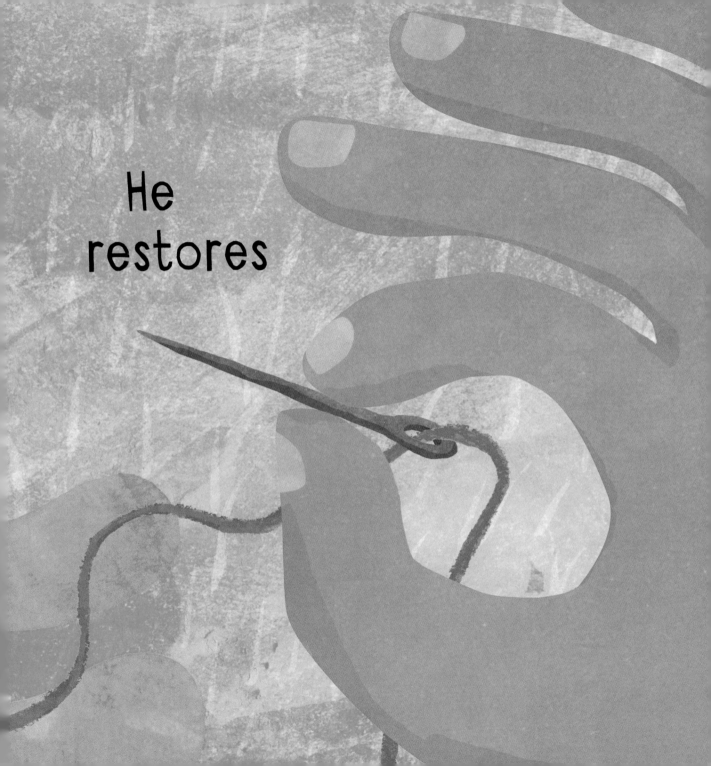

He
restores

my soul.

He guides me in the paths of righteousness for his name's sake.

Even though I walk
through the valley
of the shadow of death,
I will fear no evil,

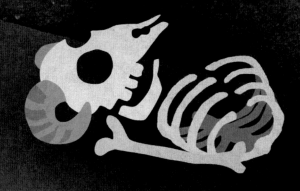

for you are
with me.

Your rod and your staff,
they comfort me.

You prepare a table before me in the presence of my enemies.

You anoint
my head
with oil.

My cup
runs over.

Surely goodness
and loving kindness
shall follow me all
the days of my life,

and I will dwell in the LORD's house forever.

I HOPE YOU ENJOYED THIS BOOK

You can find these words in the Bible in the book of Psalms. This psalm was written by King David. David became a great king, but he wasn't born into a royal family. When he was young, David had to look after his dad's sheep! His job was to keep the sheep safe and make sure they had enough to eat and drink. David called the Lord his shepherd because he knew God was taking care of him. Did you know that Jesus called himself a shepherd?

> JESUS SAID "I AM THE GOOD SHEPHERD. THE GOOD SHEPHERD LAYS DOWN HIS LIFE FOR THE SHEEP."
> JOHN 10:11

The amazing news of the Bible is that Jesus died on the cross so that God can take our sin away. Sin is anything we do that makes God unhappy – like telling lies, being selfish or hurting people. Jesus loves us so much that he took the punishment we deserve for the bad things we do. When we believe in Jesus, he forgives our sin and helps us live in a way that makes him happy. And just like a good shepherd takes care of their sheep, Jesus will guide you, protect you and be with you no matter what.

Made in the USA
Las Vegas, NV
24 February 2024

86144702R00021